MARCUS; OR THE SECRET OF SWEET

BY
TARELL ALVIN McCRANEY

★

★

DRAMATISTS
PLAY SERVICE
INC.

2

To my Best Loni and Luis

MARCUS; OR THE SECRET OF SWEET was produced at the McCarter Theatre in Princeton, New Jersey, opening on May 22, 2009. It was directed by Robert O'Hara; the set design was by James Schuette; the costume design was by Karen Perry; the lighting design was by Jane Cox; the sound design was by Lindsay Jones; and the production stage manager was Cheryl Mintz. The cast was as follows:

MARCUS .... Alano Miller
OSHA .... Kianné Muschett
SHAUNTA IYUN .... Nikiya Mathis
OBA .... Heather Alicia Simms
SHUN/ELEGUA .... Kimberly Hébert Gregory
OGUN SIZE .... Marc Damon Johnson
OSHOOSI SIZE .... Brian Tyree Henry
SHUA .... Samuel Ray Gates
TERRELL .... Brian Tyree

CHARACTERS

MARCUS ESHU, a young man of Color, son of Elegba and Oba.

OSHA, a young woman of Color, Daughter of Shun and Shango.

SHAUNTA IYUN, a young woman of Color, Daughter of Nia.

OBA, a mother of Color, mother to Marcus Eshu.

SHUN, a mother of Color, mother to Osha (to be played by the same actress as ELEGUA).

ELEGUA, an older woman of Color, aunt to Ogun Size and Oshoosi Size (to be played the same actress as SHUN).

OGUN SIZE, a man of Color, brother to Oshoosi Size.

OSHOOSI SIZE, a ghost, brother to Ogun Size.

SHUA, a young man of Color, from Up North.

TERRELL, a young dark-skinned man of Color.

PLACE

San Pere, Louisiana.

TIME

Late August (distant present).

MARCUS; OR THE SECRET OF SWEET

Prologue

Marcus Eshu lies in his bed sleeping. Dreaming.

Enter Oshoosi Size from a pool or screen of water.

He speaks directly to the audience.

OSHOOSI SIZE.
Remind him ... Tell him that one day ...
I say to him one day. I walk up on him
He working on something ... I say I'm
Finna drive this truck. He must've been
'Bout eleven hell I was only seven I say to him, I
Say, "Look here man I'ma drive this here ... "
He look at me like he couldn't be bothered.
I say, "Alright." I hopped up in that
Seat. I ain't know what I was doing. Guess
He ain't know either 'til it crank up. Grrr!
Shot out from under that damn ... cut right
And say, "Nigga." Nah, now don't get all
Like that he ain't say, "Young man," he say,
"Nigga, get yo ass ... what you doing!?" I say
"I'm drivin' s'what I told you I was gone do."
Truck start to move though. I wasn't planning
On that. I'm panicking 'cause I know I can
Jump out right now but I don't want to
Leave the truck but not like I can do a damn

Thing to stop, move, turn it. I'm just seven.
Who let a seven-year-old … I feel this arm reach 'round
And sling me out the seat. I'm tumbling
But I'm okay, skin't up but okay. I see him
He cut the engine.
And everything get quiet 'til I hear
Dress/skirt rustling through high grass.
"Whap." She slapped him
So hard blood spit from his lip. Whap!
"I told you to watch him," she saying low to him.
Put her finger close up in his face turn and walk away.
And I see him break down. I see him double over,
Put his hand to his mouth and just crying. *(Oshoosi illustrates this motion.)*
He look at me.
And I realize he ain't crying 'cause she hit him.
He ain't crying cause she point her finger. He
In tears 'cause he almost didn't get me. He almost
Ain't catch me. Almost … Huh.
Remind him of that. Tell him for me … Tell him.
(Oshoosi Size sinks into the pool or fades into the screen of water. Shift.)

OBA. *(Offstage.)*
Marcus …

(Lights out on Oshoosi. Marcus wakes breathing heavy. Offstage.)
Marcus!

MARCUS.
Ma'am?

OBA. *(Offstage.)*
C'mon, we gone be late! *(Lights.)*

A Processional

The cast forms a funeral processional. Led by Ogun Size.

Terrell opens a large black umbrella, which the cast folds in various poses of mourning and cross up and offstage.

OGUN SIZE.
>   A funeral processional for a warrior lost.
>   Walk with me Lord!
>   Walk with me.
>   Walk with me Lord
>   Walk with me.
>   While I am on this …

(The cast hums sings, harmonizes with Ogun Size. Shun, held by Terrell, passes Ogun towards offstage. Osha and Shaunta walk towards Ogun.)

>   Tedious journey.
>   I want you Lord. To walk
>   With me.

(Ogun breaks down; puts his hand to his mouth, doubles over and cries to himself. He walks offstage. Marcus runs onstage just in time to see this. This stops Marcus in his tracks, he stares at Ogun. Ogun and others exit.)

ACT ONE

Scene 1

OSHA.
    Marcus?
MARCUS.
    Ever seen a black boy stop 'n' stare?
SHAUNTA IYUN.
    You coming?
MARCUS.
    Turn his head to the side …
OSHA.
    Cmon … Marcus?
MARCUS.
    Like he just heard a ghost
SHAUNTA IYUN.
    Eh Boy …
MARCUS.
    Or remembered a dream?
SHAUNTA IYUN and OSHA.
    Marcus!
MARCUS.
    I … I can't go down there.
OSHA.
    Why not?
MARCUS.
    I got this feeling.
SHAUNTA IYUN.
    Shaunta moves to leave his butt right there.
OSHA.
    Shaunta?
SHAUNTA IYUN.
    What?
OSHA.
    Describe the feeling?

MARCUS.

Strange like, like I been here before.

OSHA.

It's a funeral ...

SHAUNTA IYUN.

We all been here before.

OSHA.

Let's just go down so we get it over with.

SHAUNTA IYUN.

Osha don't pull him girl let Marcus

Foolish self sit right here if he want.

This ain't your day. This ain't his day.

This your daddy, Shango, funeral, girl c'mon.

OSHA.

No, wait, I barely know'd the n ...

SHAUNTA IYUN.

Osha!

OSHA.

Marc ...

SHAUNTA IYUN.

Here she go.

OSHA.

Osha steps to her best friend.

SHAUNTA IYUN.

Ackin' like he her boyfriend.

OSHA.

Come down.

SHAUNTA IYUN.

Boy holding us up ...

OSHA.

I need you to.

SHAUNTA IYUN.

Ain't even his people's funeral.

OSHA.

For me.

(Closer.)

MARCUS.

Marcus uncomfortable ...

Alright!

OSHA.
Alright?
SHAUNTA IYUN.
Alright. Shoot let's …
OGUN SIZE and COMPANY. *(Offstage.)*
Oh when the saints.
Oh when the saints go marching in …
Hmmm.
SHAUNTA IYUN.
Ain't this about a …
Now we done missed the damn burial.
What's wrong with you?
MARCUS.
Shaunta!
SHAUNTA IYUN.
What?
OSHA.
It's cool
SHAUNTA IYUN.
Cool where? Not out here. It's hot. Past 90 degrees
Shaunta wipes her brow.
MARCUS.
I'm sorry Osha.
OSHA.
It's alright Marcus Eshu.
SHAUNTA IYUN.
Be sorry to me too. I'm your best too.
Lord I'm in hell and I ain't even the one dead.
Sorry Osha. Shaunta pats her chest.
OSHA.
Let's just go.
SHAUNTA IYUN.
We can't go. That's your daddy they just …
OSHA.
Well we missed it.
SHAUNTA IYUN.
'Cause of Marcus.
MARCUS.
I said sorry.

SHAUNTA IYUN.
Yeah but why we up here atop this here hill
in the one when we should have followed the
Christian jubilee to the cemetery to see them set
Osha's daddy to rest.
MARCUS.
I told you I was tired.
OSHA.
You ain't say that.
MARCUS.
I.
OSHA and SHAUNTA IYUN.
I
SHAUNTA IYUN.
You was swearing it's de ja vu
MARCUS.
I said that?
OSHA.
Wow …
SHAUNTA IYUN.
You got a secret!
OSHA.
Osha smiles.
MARCUS.
No. I. It's not a secret
It's … I ain't been sleeping.
OSHA.
Why?
SHAUNTA IYUN.
Oba got you working the late shift.
MARCUS.
If you don't … get outta my face.
OSHA.
Marcus what's the secret.
MARCUS.
Ain't no secret. I'm just dreaming.
OSHA.
Huh. Like sweet dreams?
SHAUNTA IYUN.
Or beautiful nightmares?

MARCUS.
    Just a dream ...
SHAUNTA IYUN.
    What's in it?
OSHA.
    Who in it?

Scene 2

SHUN.
    Osha!
SHAUNTA IYUN.
    Ms. Shun!
OSHA.
    Mother of Osha ...
MARCUS.
    She can't stand Marcus.
SHUN.
    Shun enters
    Staring at her daughter like, "She must've lost her,"
    Through clenched teeth, "Motherfuckinmind!"
    Girl! How many times, too many, have I
    Told you to stay away from hanging as you
    Calls it with that boy, sweet Marcus, huh!
MARCUS.
    See.
SHUN.
    That's all I ask.
    That's all I say. See him in school, at home
    Hang with your other girlfriends. I says it time
    And time a ... But I look up and here you go
    Again down the way from the ceremony putting
    Your fallen father in the fucking floor and you
    Sitting here sipping on time and sunshine with
    Candy Marcus! Lord! If it ain't one thing it's
    Another. Osha, girl, if you don't get your ass over here!
    Ooh!

OSHA.

> Kisses her teeth
> Stch
> I gotta go y'all, she trippin'.

SHUN.

> Oh I'm trippin' huh, I'm falling? You wait
> 'til we get to this house Osha see how fast
> I can get down. Exit Shun holding hard to
> Her stubborn child, I done told you he just
> like his dead damn daddy.

Scene 3

SHAUNTA IYUN.

> Forgive her Marcus. She buried her man today.

MARCUS.

> I'm used to it.

SHAUNTA IYUN.

> Too used to it.

MARCUS.

> She been saying since …

SHAUNTA IYUN.

> Is it true?

MARCUS.

> I'm like my daddy?

SHAUNTA IYUN.

> Was he sweet?

MARCUS.

> What!

SHAUNTA IYUN.

> Are you sweet Marcus Eshu?

MARCUS.

> I don't? How you just gone … I mean my daddy's dead.

SHAUNTA IYUN.

> But you're here. You alive.
> Are you sweet?
> Marcus.

Marcus?

MARCUS.

I heard you Shaunta Iyun!

SHAUNTA IYUN.

It look heavy. Like it's hard on your heart.
Share that burden brother.
Shaunta sits next to her friend.
I couldn't either, I guess, after somebody called me
All kinds of out my name like that. Hard to say
Yeah that's me that's what I am that nasty thing
She wrinkled up her face to say.

MARCUS.

Huh.

SHAUNTA IYUN.

Seem like you ain't never gone confess it.
Surely not to Osha. You know she like you,
Huh? You know she think, "We best friends
Better lovers!" I ain't Osha. I am just your
Friend. You can tell me.

MARCUS.

Wonder where that come from, calling somebody sweet?

SHAUNTA IYUN.

They passed it down to us!

MARCUS.

What?

SHAUNTA IYUN.

Black MoPhobia.

MARCUS.

Girl you crazy …

SHAUNTA IYUN.

Passed down from slavery.
Say the slaveowners get pissed if they find
Out they slaves got gay love.
That means less children, less slaves … less.

MARCUS.

Shaunta …

SHAUNTA IYUN.

Think about it Marcus … Where else it come from?
We just naturally mad at gay folk? Come on!
Imagine it, how they got "down back then?

16

'Round here niggas think they got it hard on the "down low."

MARCUS.

Don't say that word …

SHAUNTA IYUN.

What about back then?
Two slaves one dark, and one light, one house
And the other field. They see each other one day.
That sparkle in they eye, they begin to gather
Together when they can, hide their love from the light.
Dark kisses in the midnight hour, with shackles for love
Bracelets, chains for promise rings. One night
Master come up on them in their secret spot 'cause
Some handkerchief-head other slave, jealous or holy, went
Off and told, "I seen't so and so house and so and so field
Slave down together in the quarter."

MARCUS.

You think slaves was snitchin'?

SHAUNTA IYUN.

Nosiness is primordial, snitching inevitable.

MARCUS.

Huh.

SHAUNTA IYUN.

Master tie and tether the lovers in front of e'rybody,
Talking 'bout, "sending a message." Placing weights
On their private portions. Lashing into the skin that they just held
To tight moments ago. Skin that was just kissed now
Split ope' from th' slash of dis white man hands
When the wounds right he run down get some sugar
Prolly pour it on so it sting not as bad as salt but it get Sticky
Melt in the singing Southern sun. Sweetness draw all the
Bugs and infection to the sores … sweetness harder to wash.
It
Become molasses in all that heat and blood and …

MARCUS.

Marcus draws air …

SHAUNTA IYUN.

That's what you dreaming about, Marcus?
That's what got you waking up sweating?
You wake up scared that somebody gone catch on or …

MARCUS.

    I wake up missing my daddy.

SHAUNTA IYUN.

    You see him

    In your dream?

MARCUS.

    No, that's how I know I miss him.

SHAUNTA IYUN.

    Shaunta leaves it for now.

    Alright Marc, alright.

Scene 4

OBA.

    Marcus! Marcus …

    Enter Oba calling for her son …

MARCUS.

    Whom she babies …

OBA.

    Marcus!

MARCUS.

    Yes, Mama?

OBA.

    Baby …

MARCUS.

OBA.

    Where you been? I was up and down

    Looking for you.

MARCUS.

    Sorry, I didn't feel like going to the grave.

OBA.

    Why, what's wrong baby?

MARCUS.

    I got this …

    Mama, stop calling me baby.

OBA.

    But you my baby

MARCUS.
Mama …
OBA.
Marcus, you feeling alright? You got up
Two three times in the night last night.
You having movements?
MARCUS.
Tell me about my daddy.
OBA.
Oba's face.
Huh.
The Father is in heaven and all is right
MARCUS.
No, Mama, I know all that. The Bible talks to
Me about all that But I'm talking 'bout my real
Daddy. Tell me 'bout 'Legba.
OBA.
Why?
MARCUS.
'Cause I'm asking. 'Cause you never do.
OBA.
Ooh, it's hot out here, let's go.
MARCUS.
It's always hot. You notice that every summer
Same reason it gets hot.
Shrugs.
OBA.
Have you … Who you talking to?
MARCUS.
Ma'am, sorry, I'm just saying every time we get near
'Bout this conversation it gets hot or the meter
Running or the chickens burning. All the time,
Every time, something starts to happen too long
When I mention the name Elegba.
OBA.
Huh …
MARCUS.
I just want to know about him.
OBA.
What you need to know?

MARCUS.

Am I ... like him?

OBA.

Some traits we gets from our peoples are
Sleeping ...

MARCUS.

The way I act.

OBA.

Sometimes it's better to let sleeping traits lie.

MARCUS.

Was he ...

OBA.

What, Marcus, What?

MARCUS.

OBA.

Oba looks to the ground. Lord.

MARCUS.

Mama I ...

OBA.

I tell you this Marcus. I don't know what all the
Sudden got you on this search to find out your father
But if it's got relation to the reason why you locked
In the bathroom but not using it ...
Or that long stare I see you, I see you, giving over
Eric down the way you best pray on it. Think to it.
Some things are better buried! Some things left better
Unsaid! Ain't nothing sweet about a soft son!
She takes a breath.
Pick your face up off the floor, baby, and let's go.

MARCUS.

I'm gonna ... I'm gonna walk.

OBA.

Huh. She leans in. You find your way home tonight.
When you come in you make sure you check that li'l
Funky attitude at the door. You got school tomorrow.
Senior year or not. Funeral or none. Oba exits.

A Daydream

MARCUS.
I ... *(Sighs.)*
Ever had so much on your mind you forget what
You wanted to think about?
That's when it's dangerous.
Your mind starts playing on those
Things you want least to wander
Like school.
Like Latin.
Starting the second year in that class
And it's impossible to focus.

TERRELL.
Enter

TERRELL and SHUA.
The boyz.

MARCUS.
In this class of language there are boys from
All the teams. Focus.

TERRELL.
They sit behind Marcus.

MARCUS.
From basketball to track, varsity to junior.

TERRELL.
Whispering:
Marcus!

MARCUS.
And every Monday while the pop quizzes line
The desks.

TERRELL.
Eh Marcus!

MARCUS.
The boys all lean in a li'l closer.

SHUA.
Ssp!

MARCUS.

Trying to pick up the answers that Marcus slinging
Down.

TERRELL.

Marcus Eshu ...

MARCUS.

They make propositions.

TERRELL.

Eh ...

MARCUS.

Whisper in hushed teacher-can't-hear tones.

SHUA.

Let me see!

MARCUS.

Their heads yank and mouths smile.

TERRELL.

Marc ...

MARCUS.

Motioning for me to move my head ...

TERRELL.

Move your hand ...

SHUA and TERRELL.

Move!

MARCUS.

Whispering ...

TERRELL.

Marcus ... Marcus!

MARCUS.

Focus.

TERRELL.

But see all they want are the answers to
The test ...

MARCUS.

Focus ...

TERRELL.

Answers that will make it easier to get back to track and field
...

MARCUS.

Focus ...

TERRELL.
But Marcus' mind is wishin' their heads were yanking and
Their mouths were asking ...
MARCUS.
Focus Marcus ...
TERRELL.
To let me come over ...
MARCUS.
Focus.
SHUA.
Let me step closer ...
MARCUS.
Focus.
MARCUS, TERRELL and SHUA.
Let me!
TERRELL.
Terrell and the boys fade
Like an early evening mirage.

Scene 5

ELEGUA.
Enter Elegua walking as fast as she can for near 70.
She runs into ...
(Marcus staring offstage.)
Move boy.
MARCUS.
Ms. Elegua.
Marcus moves his hand to hide his ...
ELEGUA.
Huh. She moves. Sick ... Sick ...
MARCUS.
Ma'am!
ELEGUA.
To death of funerals. Sick of 'em. I'm down there
Trying to pay respect to the fallen soldier and these
People having an argument ova' who was his better friend.

I say, don't seem like none of you too good 'cause while
He was off in the war y'all was over here trying to get his girl.
But I ain't say much, see, that's when I turns to Ogun I say …
MARCUS.
Ogun's down there still …
ELEGUA.
"Yeah chile." I say,
She hits the air
"'Ey let's go." "Okay." He standing there
Crying his one last cry. Lord!
MARCUS.
He coming back?
ELEGUA.
Who cares! I know, I ain't going to no more funerals with his
Crying ass. Making all that …
MARCUS.
He takin' it hard?
ELEGUA.
Eh what the … I know Oba raised you better than to
Keep cutting off elders.
MARCUS.
Marcus apologetic.
ELEGUA.
Aw shit boy you near 'bout grown you ain't suppose
To let me get away with that. Yeah, he taking it hard.
That's what he do, take everything to heart since
Oshoosi left.
MARCUS.
Who?
ELEGUA.
Ogun's brother.
MARCUS.
ELEGUA.
Your daddy's best …
MARCUS.
Marcus shakes his head.
ELEGUA.
Now wait a minute
This ain't no Keith Sweat song; where you
Say no n I say yes. Your daddy's best was Oshoosi, Ogun's

Brother. How you don't know that?

MARCUS.

It's a lot I don't know.

ELEGUA.

Huh, I bet it ain't, wait.

MARCUS.

What I'm waiting on?

ELEGUA.

Hmmm huh. Well I wish I had the time patience
Or want withal to fill you in fella but I gots to go
This here heat make your titties sag further south
Than Violet.

MARCUS.

Wait! Please …
I … *(Sighs.)*

ELEGUA.

It's alright boi. Sometimes your mouth the last
Place words wanna go …

MARCUS.

Was he sweet?

ELEGUA.

Good evening to you too.

MARCUS.

Heavy breath.
Was my daddy sweet?

ELEGUA.

Ask your mama.

MARCUS.

When I do she …

ELEGUA.

Throw it off talk about something else.

MARCUS.

Yeah.

ELEGUA.

Your daddy liked girls enough to have you
That ain't enough for you?

MARCUS.

Yeah but …

ELEGUA.

Listen if'n you looking for them black or white

Wrong or right answers from me honey you got
The wrong one. I just point out to you the obvious
And hope like hell you stop questioning me 'bout
Things I don't even much know how to explain.

MARCUS.

You know how to explain dreams?

ELEGUA.

Huh.

MARCUS.

I saw Ogun crying.

ELEGUA.

Huh.

MARCUS.

And it reminded me of this dream I keep having ...

ELEGUA.

When your daddy was little,
He run around here talking about his dreams.
And at the time ... At the time all seem right with it.
Every now and then somebody catch the number off
Something he say but it ain't never catch hold of nothing
Serious. And then one day, one ... huh.

MARCUS.

Ms. Elegua?

ELEGUA.

Go 'head tell me your dream.

MARCUS.

All of it?

ELEGUA.

Nah everything but the good part.

MARCUS.

Okay. Okay.
There is this man. He always he saying things to
Me. Sometimes in the rain. Light at first
Then so hard I can barely hear. Hard rain.
Rain so hard it look like it's coming from the
Ground it's hitting that hard. He keep ...
He keep telling me ... Things ...

ELEGUA.

MARCUS.

You okay?

ELEGUA.

Fine. What he saying? I' th' dream, huh?

MARCUS.

I 'on't remember when I wake up.

OGUN SIZE. *(Offstage.)*

Aunt Elegua!

ELEGUA.

Elegua straightens up.

You ain't never seen him before?

MARCUS.

No.

ELEGUA.

And he ain't trying to freak you like you like it?

MARCUS.

No.

ELEGUA.

You want him to?

MARCUS.

Maybe.

ELEGUA.

Huh.

MARCUS.

What?

ELEGUA.

Shhh!

Keep listening to the man in your dreams.

Scene 6

OGUN SIZE.

Ogun Size enters. Aunt Elegua!

Calling for his aunt. Elegua!

ELEGUA.

I hear you. You see I'm standing right

Here.

OGUN SIZE.

Where'd you go?

27

Y'all alright?

ELEGUA.

Fine.

MARCUS.

Huh.

OGUN SIZE.

What you, what you two up to?

ELEGUA.

Nothing.

MARCUS.

Uh uh.

OGUN SIZE.

Uh Huh.

ELEGUA.

We was just talking about old times.

MARCUS.

Old times.

ELEGUA.

I was just telling Marcus here …

MARCUS.

She was telling me …

ELEGUA.

How you and Oshoosi and his daddy were friends.

OGUN SIZE.

I mean we wasn't friends …

I mean he and Shoosi were …

MARCUS.

So you knew my daddy Ogun?

OGUN SIZE.

Yeah I knew him … but he was …

ELEGUA.

Close.

MARCUS.

Close?

OGUN SIZE.

Close to my brother … My brother Oshoosi.

They was …

Marcus how you getting home?

ELEGUA.

Reckon the same way he got here!

MARCUS.

What you mean close?

OGUN SIZE.

Nothing.

ELEGUA.

Swat. Eh!

You need to worry 'bout your ailing auntie who

Getting tapped like a natural resource by these

Lisquitos! Swat.

OGUN SIZE.

Oh ... I'm sorry Aunt Ele' you ready to go.

ELEGUA.

Nah I'm sitting here hitting myself 'cause I'm

Into it! C'mon here!

OGUN SIZE.

You sure you don't want a ride home Marcus?

ELEGUA.

Elegua shaking her head. Let it 'lone now.

MARCUS.

Thank you. I'ma walk.

Marcus looks to the sky.

ELEGUA.

Gone 'head Marcus. Keep your head up.

Out the side of her mouth.

Hold to that dream.

A Mirage

MARCUS.
> Wanna watch while I try and put two and two
> And get more than four? What in the world was
> She talking about? I don't mean to mock but ...
> "Hold to that dream?" Huh. In that dream, though
> When I'm sleep I feel it, right before I get where
> It's going, right before it makes all the sense ... I wake
> Up and it's like all the pieces scatter. Like the sun burn
> Out the fog and the smoke and I can't make sense of
> It no more. It's just pieces, parts. 'Hold to that dream.'
> Maybe if I put back the pieces. All I remember of that
> Dream is ... light and water and a man. And there
> In the sky is the moon, and if I walk a li'l further
> I'll find water ... maybe even the man
> Stupid ... No ... shrugs. Huh. Maybe I find ... Huh.
> Marcus moves.

Scene 7

SHAUNTA IYUN.
> Shaunta Iyun enters calling for her friend
> Marcus!
MARCUS.
> Eh, Shaunta!
SHAUNTA IYUN.
> Marcus, where you been?
MARCUS.
> The funeral.
SHAUNTA IYUN.
> You ain't been home.
MARCUS.
> Nope.

SHAUNTA IYUN.
    Ain't you …
MARCUS.
    Marcus moves.
SHAUNTA IYUN.
    Where the hell you going?
MARCUS.
    Following my dream
    It's always near the water and …
SHAUNTA IYUN.
    Uh Marcus …
MARCUS.
    I'm headed near the bayou. Wanna come?
SHAUNTA IYUN.
    It's dark!
MARCUS.
    So that mean, no?
    Marcus moves to …
SHAUNTA IYUN.
    Wait … uh Marcus
MARCUS.
    Huh?
SHAUNTA IYUN.
    What star is that near the moon?
MARCUS.
    Venus.
SHAUNTA IYUN.
    Oh.
    And what's the closest planet to the sun?
MARCUS.
    Mercury.
SHAUNTA IYUN.
    Thanks and are you sweet?
MARCUS.
    What!
SHAUNTA IYUN.
    Damnit … almost.
MARCUS.
    Shaunta!

SHAUNTA IYUN.
    I let you off easy earlier but come
    On now. We got to talk about this.
MARCUS.
    Why?
SHAUNTA IYUN.
    Because I wanna know.
MARCUS.
    Stop wanting ...
SHAUNTA IYUN.
    And you need to say it.
MARCUS.
    Marcus looks away.
SHAUNTA IYUN.
    Marcus you out here at this hour chasing
    A dream? What? Huh. Why?
    What you trying to find? What you running
    Away from?
MARCUS.
    I ain't running from ...
    I told you there is ... keeping me up.
    I mean I ain't scared but it's sad you know.
    I feel like there's somebody crying. I told it to
    Ms. Elegua and she say ...
SHAUNTA IYUN.
    Wait a minute.
MARCUS.
    It's got all this rain in it ...
SHAUNTA IYUN.
    Ms. Elegua!
MARCUS.
    And this man that I don't know ...
SHAUNTA IYUN.
    That's the same lady who used to chase
    Osha around the projects with a lighter
    Talking 'bout, "I burn your coochie hairs!"
MARCUS.
    I know ...
SHAUNTA IYUN.
    This the same lady who smell like Dewar's

White Label at communion.
MARCUS.
Shaunta Iyun …
SHAUNTA IYUN.
The same chick …
MARCUS.
This ain't about her. She say if I'm a if
I … you know …
She say my daddy used to dream too.
That his dreams meant something. Maybe
Mine do too.
SHAUNTA IYUN.
What?

Scene 8

OBA. *(Offstage.)*
Marcus!
MARCUS.
Oh shit it's my mama!
OBA.
Marcus Eshu!
Oba enters
Marcus!
Calling for her son …
MARCUS.
Shaunta Iyun…?
SHAUNTA IYUN.
No.
MARCUS.
Please!?
SHAUNTA IYUN.
Lord!
MARCUS.
Marcus hides in the night.
OBA.
Hey Shaunta.

SHAUNTA IYUN.

    Ms. Oba how you?

OBA.

    Good. You seen Marcus?

SHAUNTA IYUN.

    Yeah.

MARCUS.

OBA.

    Where is he?

SHAUNTA IYUN.

    Oh, I don't know.

OBA.

    I thought you said you seen him.

SHAUNTA IYUN.

    Earlier today, at the funeral.

OBA.

    Huh.

SHAUNTA IYUN.

    Sad funeral.

OBA.

    Oh yeah it was.

SHAUNTA IYUN.

    I mean I ain't one to cry but Shango was
    Such a hero, you know? Going off to fight
    That fight in Iraq.

OBA.

    It's true.

SHAUNTA IYUN.

    They say that fighting in the Middle East
    Ain't neva gone stop Ms. Oba what you
    think?

OBA.

    Well ...

SHAUNTA IYUN.

    I mean they been fighting like that since
    The times of Abraham. Ain't neva been
    Peace between them. You a Bible-beating
    Woman you know.

OBA.

    Hold on Shaunta ...

SHAUNTA IYUN.

Oh I'm sorry did I say that out loud?

OBA.

Yes you did!

SHAUNTA IYUN.

You know my mama raised me to speak
My mind. You raise Marcus like that?

OBA.

I told Marcus …

SHAUNTA IYUN.

'Cause he seem like he always scared to
Say how he really feel. He ever come to
You and tell you some secret about him?

OBA.

Um. No. I mean not since he was a child.

SHAUNTA IYUN.

But if Marcus told you something …
Something was hurting his heart, you would
Listen right? You would hear him.

OBA.

Huh. Why you … you know some secret about
Marcus?

SHAUNTA IYUN.

Oh. Oh no I was just asking. I mean … he
My best friend but he can be so secretive
Sometimes. Once he told me that he thought
Maybe he had dreams …

OBA.

Dreams?

SHAUNTA IYUN.

Yeah, yeah like his daddy.

OBA.

To herself
I wonder which dream his daddy give 'em.

SHAUNTA IYUN.

Ma'am?

OBA.

Nothing. Let me go find this boy.

SHAUNTA IYUN.

So loud.

Oh alright. You be careful Ms. Oba
AND IF I SEE MARCUS TONIGHT I WILL
Make sure to tell him you say, GET
HOME NOW.

OBA.

Uh Thank you … Shaunta. Yeah.
Oba exits.

MARCUS.

Marcus, nods to his friend.

SHAUNTA IYUN.

She smiles.

MARCUS.

Marcus exits.

Scene 9

There is a noise heard offstage like a gunshot or loud fireworks.

SHAUNTA IYUN.

Marcus!

OSHA.

Enter Osha.
Walking fast.
(The sound again!)
Her breath comes loose …

SHAUNTA IYUN.

She holds her stomach …

OSHA.

She catches her knee …

SHAUNTA IYUN and OSHA.

She …

TERRELL.

Enter Terrell laughing his ass off.
Damn what's wrong with y'all?

OSHA.

Somebody out here …

SHAUNTA IYUN.
> Shooting!

TERRELL.
> Huh. And what you come out here
> To do Shaunta Iyun eat him?

OSHA.
> What you doing out here?

TERRELL.
> Shooting fireworks

OSHA.
> That was your …

SHAUNTA IYUN.
> Stupid ass.
> What the hell you lighting fireworks for?

OSHA.
> It ain't the Fourth.

SHAUNTA IYUN.
> It's near 'bout September!

OSHA.
> Who called Marcus' name?

SHAUNTA IYUN.
> I did girl I thought he was here and …

OSHA.
> Don't even say it. Where he at?

SHAUNTA IYUN.
> Went out by the waters. Talking 'bout
> That dream and Elegua … Talking crazy
> gurl.

OSHA.
> This time a night? It's near 'bout
> Morning! What's on his mind?

TERRELL.
> Probably some dick.

OSHA.
> Eh!

SHAUNTA IYUN.
> Silly nigga!

TERRELL.
> Osha gurl, I'm saying why you
> Be gay chasing that nigga, Marcus?

OSHA.

First of all …

TERRELL.

You gone end up on Oprah I'm telling you.

OSHA.

Marcus is just sensitive …

SHAUNTA IYUN.

… And sweet.

OSHA.

Right.

You wouldn't know nothing 'bout that …

SHAUNTA IYUN.

Or a bath.

OSHA.

Dirty butt.

TERRELL.

Y'all gone catch a whole lotta hell running behind
That homo.

SHAUNTA IYUN.

Least we ain't gone catch the yit-yit running behind yo ass.

TERRELL.

Shaunta you don't run nowhere.
If you did we all feel you coming.
Ain't that what Shaunta mean
In the Cherokee? "Girl-Who-Run-Like
Thunder?"

SHAUNTA IYUN.

Osha … Shaunta Iyun calls
To her friend, Osha girl! You
Hear something?

OSHA.

What?

SHAUNTA IYUN.

Who?

Shaunta feels around in the dark.
She slaps Terrell on the face.

TERRELL.

Eh gurl!

SHAUNTA IYUN.

Oh Terrell that's yo black ass.

Damn boi you better wear bright
Colors this time of night.

TERRELL.

Whatever heifer!

SHAUNTA IYUN.

I'm just saying you better open
Your eyes bright or smile the one.
I lost you completely, soot. Thought
The Devil was calling for me. Made
Me wanna holla throw up both my
hands.

OSHA.

Girl Me too!
A gunshot is heard.

(Pah.)

TERRELL.

Wasn't me.

SHAUNTA IYUN.

Lord …

OSHA.

Where you say he went?

SHAUNTA IYUN.

C'mon let's go see.

TERRELL.

See, that's how bitches get kilt 'round
Here, investigating shit. Just like the
White folks in the scary movies they
Hear the strange noise and they got to
Go deeper in the woods 'n' shit. "No
Lil white skinny girl don't go in that
Dark basement!" Hannibal, Freddie,
Jason in the cellar playing the *Carmina
Burana* haunting music with his dick
Tucked 'tween his legs he 'bout to come
For you gurl, run! Nope, she just
Standing there calling for her friend.
Terrell gives his best Jodie Foster or
Jamie Lee, "Mike, you there." She don't
Feel it 'til it's too late. Don't sense nothing
'Til wicked man done sliced her up and through

Uh huh. Y'all go 'head and keep on
Wanting to see what's happening.
End up snoting like them white girls
In scary movies. Talking 'bout, "I'm so
Scared."
SHAUNTA IYUN.
OSHA.
SHAUNTA IYUN.
Right behind you girl.
You ready girl?
OSHA.
Right behind you girl.
TERRELL.
Damn Osha gurl da summer
Done been good to you! Lawd
Shawty! Wait up! Terrell exits
In pursuit of that ass.

Scene 10

MARCUS.
Marcus on Ms. Elegua's porch.
He starts to knock but …
ELEGUA.
Hey there.
MARCUS.
You heard me?
ELEGUA.
You walk hard.
Think you think this a catwalk or something.
MARCUS.
You always …
ELEGUA.
Calling you out?
You need something?
MARCUS.
I was headed to the waters. But I wanted to ask …
I don't mean to be …

40

ELEGUA.

    Boy stop worrying 'bout disrespecting folks … keep

    That mess up see if you don't have ulcers all up and through

    Your prostrate.

MARCUS.

    Earlier,

    You were going to tell me something else.

ELEGUA.

    I don't wanna talk. I'm tired.

MARCUS.

    Ma'am I know you old and prolly …

ELEGUA.

    Call me old one more 'gin.

MARCUS.

    Let me finish.

ELEGUA.

MARCUS.

    I'm just confused. I mean why my daddy dreams made

    You sad? What 'bout my dreams make you get quiet?

ELEGUA.

    Heavy breath.

    Used to be people come listen to a boy like

    You. Say boys like you, with sensibility like

    Yourn, with, what they call, Ralph Tresvant Sensitivity,

    Elegua shakes her hand slow like she holding a tambourine.

    Say he have a gift to see things we all can't. Hear

    Messages and things we can't quite.

MARCUS.

    ELEGUA.

    Say sweet boys got a secret of sight.

MARCUS.

    I'm not …

ELEGUA.

    You marched your li'l light-skin self all the way over here

    To lie?

MARCUS.

    I mean … who said …

ELEGUA.

    Folks before your time.

MARCUS.

Huh that's crazy.

ELEGUA.

'Fore my time.

MARCUS.

Stch they ain't even have gay folks in Africa.

ELEGUA.

Huh.

Don't let 'em fool you all your life.

MARCUS.

So, my dream mean I'm ... sweet?

ELEGUA.

Gone boy ...

MARCUS.

I mean what? That's it! What about the man?

ELEGUA.

I said ...

MARCUS.

And all that rain ...

ELEGUA.

GONE!

Elegua trembling. Barely holding herself together.

Please ... I don't know all. I don't. But all that rain?

And 'nese people round here talking 'bout a storm coming.

That dream ... That dream,

It can't mean good. Just can't.

MARCUS.

Marcus fades off her porch.

Scene 11

SHAUNTA IYUN.
    STOP FOLLOWING US!
TERRELL.
    Whoop, whoop pull over that ass too fat.
SHAUNTA IYUN.
    You know I hate you?
TERRELL.
    The feeling's reciprocal.
SHAUNTA IYUN.
    Shaunta shocked
    Oh hell nah!
OSHA.
    Boi you learning words?
TERRELL.
    Reciprocal comes from the word reciprocus
    Re: meaning back pro meaning forward.
    Right now we need to re pro out this damn
    Off road.
OSHA.
Not 'til we find Marcus.
TERRELL.
    It's dark as hell out here.
    She know where she going?
SHAUNTA IYUN.
    Hmhuh.
TERRELL.
    How the hell? 'Cause she got them pretty eyes they
    Can see everything.
OSHA.
    Oh. Hey … boy …
TERRELL.
    Yeah …
    So where we wandering?
SHAUNTA IYUN.
    To the spot her 'n Marcus first kiss.

TERRELL.

Euh!

OSHA.

Dag Shaunta!

TERRELL.

Out here?

SHAUNTA IYUN.

They were nine.

OSHA.

Its was just a …

SHAUNTA IYUN.

First n last.

OSHA.

It was our favorite spot

SHAUNTA IYUN.

Was …

OSHA.

C'mon y'all walk up.

Spirit in the Dark

MARCUS.
    Trust. I know. Ain't no answers out here. Not to
    Me particular
    Just sky and dust but ain't we all?
    Don't you wish it was?
    Don't you wish the days, all damn day, running into
    Everything that scares the ... Outta you would just wash
    Out into the waters, drain away. That the disappointed,
    You-strange-boy stares would light up and leave-like, not
    Look down on you wondering, "What you doing?
    What you thinking? What you dreaming?" 'Specially when
    'On't know yo ownself. Looking at you like you a problem
    Staring at you like, "Where your shame?"
    Right when everything seems simple. I might be ...
    Or at least it might be alright to be ... here come some
    secret.
    Some dream.
    And you just smile and
    Smile. You know that feeling? To just smile and smile and
    Smile and smile and smile and smile and ... when you wanna
    Just get up on table-tops and scream you want to say, say ...
    huh
    Huh.
    It's nice out here, you think? The bayou. Maybe it's magic
    out
    Here. I always thought so ... Magic. "Secret of sight." More
    like
    The ... more like the secret of sweet. The secret is ain't
    nobody
    Think it's a secret 'cept me, 'cept those who don't want to
    see.
    And those who do keep talking 'bout me saying things to me
    Man even my own dreams won't let me ... these the times
    You wish for a daddy, maybe not, maybe he wouldn't be
    proud of

Me … but at least you can scream at somebody you can …
stand up
To 'em and tell him tell how it hurt you to be … say "I ain't
Put this black skin on me I didn't press these … boy-boy
Thoughts into my head." You think I set out to be dreaming
o' dis
Man
Old
Enough
To be my … you
Talking to me slowly i' th' water 'n' rain crying, laughing
Singing sometimes all in the rain. I didn't make him up I
ain't
Conjure him to me. All I am is here
Heard, here so … so you don't got to understand me 'cause I
don't
I don't hardly either just … just love me.
You ever wish it would all just wash away?
Never heard
A black boy say that I bet. Not out loud.
But I do. I do. I wish wish them waters would
Rise up like that water in my dreams
And take it all me too, out and away. You
Wish that sometimes? I do. I do.

Scene 12

OGUN SIZE.
    Be careful what you wish for Marcus.
    Enter Ogun Size
MARCUS.
    Marcus moves.
OGUN SIZE.
    Where you going?
MARCUS.
    I don't know.
OGUN SIZE.

I hope not closer out there to that water.

MARCUS.

Nah … I can't even swim.

OGUN SIZE.

Laughing.

Me neither. So we both be outta luck.

MARCUS.

What you doing out here?

OGUN SIZE.

Good evening to you too.

MARCUS.

I'm sorry I mean how you …

OGUN SIZE.

Nah, you ain't got to apologize …

Something caught in your eye Marcus.

Ogun wipes a tear.

MARCUS.

Thank you.

OGUN SIZE.

You ain't alright so what ailing you?

MARCUS.

Been one of them days.

OGUN SIZE.

I hear you man. Three times a charm they say.

Third time I done put down somebody who ought

To be burying me. Three times of saying Goodbye

When your daddy died …

MARCUS.

Why everybody do that?

Stop up like when they coming to tell me about …

OGUN SIZE.

You know folks, me too, you trying to explain something

You ain't never really understood. You shut up for fear of put-

ting

It wrong.

MARCUS.

Was he … sweet?

OGUN SIZE.

He could be.

MARCUS.

No I mean …

OGUN SIZE.

Interrupting

But he could be as mean as the devil too. Like every man

We all got the ability of being a lot, but you seeing that,

Sure.

MARCUS.

Huh.

OGUN SIZE.

Sit a while, hause.

MARCUS.

Alright.

OGUN SIZE.

You a lot like them, my brother your daddy.

Feel everything don't you? I ain't felt nothing 'til I

Saw you standing there staring at me at that

Funeral today.

MARCUS.

You saw me?

OGUN SIZE.

Felt like the world push up to my feet.

MARCUS.

You mean come from under …

OGUN SIZE.

No I mean I finally felt the ground.

MARCUS.

OGUN SIZE.

Memories, right they wash over you out here.

MARCUS.

Where's your brother now, Ogun?

OGUN SIZE.

Shit I don't know … 'Scuse me, son but a

Situation happened with him and

Your daddy; they got in trouble good with the

Law and

Um well I … It was me who … I asked him …

To leave town. Told him

He better if he left. Nigga never listen to

A word I say. Why he start that day I never

Know. Your daddy ... he turned hisself in.
Walked hisself right into jail one day. Guess
Without ... Without Oshoosi ...
MARCUS.
And that's where he died.
OGUN SIZE.
Yeah that's where they say 'Legba died. In jail.
He wasn't the same after Oshoosi left.
They was always together those t ...
MARCUS.
Please don't ... just tell me about them.
OGUN SIZE.
They ... huh ... it's hard to tell. 'Cause they ...
They was always made some people uncomfortable
I can't lie make my stomach funny talking 'bout it ...
But some people in this world they just fit right.
... My brother couldn't never sleep. He always had bad
dreams.
Used to piss me off. Waking up dreaming
Crying, wanting to stay up. Got so I started ignoring him. I would
hear him awake and act like I'm sleep or something. Act like
I ain't paying attention. One night 'Legba your daddy was spending
the night over they was 'bout your age. Shoosi wake up crying.
I thought he gone embarrass hisself crying in front of company.
I heard Elegba say I heard him say whisper, "Shhh! Shhh! It's gone Be
Okay. Shhh, now, Oshoosi it's gone be alright." And he stop
crying. I heard him not saying Anything. And I turned over
to see What they was doing. See what he had done to make
him stop. And Elegba had done hugged Oshoosi
Close and they had laid back down again.
I didn't know what to say. Still don't.
The next morning, I say you two niggas get y'all ass up.
Huh.
I was mad.

MARCUS.
    Why?
OGUN SIZE.
    All my life I tried to get my brother to quit crying and
    Sleep like that and never could. Never could.
MARCUS.
    You got something in your eye, Ogun.
    Marcus wipes a tear.
OGUN SIZE.
    Look at us both out here crying.
MARCUS.
    Least we crying together 'stead of separate.
    He smiles.
OGUN SIZE.
MARCUS.
    He don't know why?
OGUN SIZE.
    He smiles back.
OGUN SIZE and MARCUS.
    He ...

Scene 13

TERRELL.
    Oh y'all niggas gay!
    Enter Terrell ...
OSHA.
    With Osha girl
SHAUNTA IYUN.
    And Shaunta Iyun.
TERRELL.
    They was kissing!
SHAUNTA IYUN.
    Shut up ...
    Mr. Ogun.
MARCUS.
    Wait ...

SHAUNTA IYUN.
　　You gay?
OGUN SIZE.
　　Laughing.
　　No … I'm too old to be gay …
SHAUNTA IYUN.
　　You was kissing!
MARCUS.
　　Marcus braving.
　　I kissed him.
OGUN SIZE.
　　Too sad to be gay …
OSHA.
　　You what?
OGUN SIZE.
　　Too …
　　TERRELL.
　　He sweet …
MARCUS.
　　Shut up …
　　TERRELL.
　　You gay … what …
　　Ray Charles can see that
　　And he blind and dead.
SHAUNTA IYUN.
　　And you couldn't tell me …
MARCUS.
　　Osha …
OSHA.
　　You know I love you?
MARCUS.
　　I love you …
SHAUNTA IYUN.
　　But like a friend.
OSHA.
　　Osha's face …
SHAUNTA IYUN.
　　Falls into the water.
OSHA.
Exit Osha.

OGUN SIZE.
I'm sorry Marcus.
> TERRELL.
>> Y'all finna kiss again?
SHAUNTA IYUN, MARCUS, OGUN and OSHA.
> SHUT UP!
OSHA.
> Enter Osha … Marcus!
> Calling for her friend.
> Marcus Eshu!
> Do you know how many niggas would
> Stomp a hole in heaven to get with me
> You telling me you rather be with him?
OGUN SIZE.
> No!
OSHA.
> Gay or no he old and I'm phyne!
TERRELL.
> Yes Lord.
OSHA.
> They all stare at Terrell.
TERRELL.
> To himself
> Shut. Up.
OSHA.
> Marcus be my friend
MARCUS.
> I am …
OSHA.
> Tell me the truth.
MARCUS.
> I do.
OSHA.
> Them dreams you was talking 'bout before
> They about a man, huh.
MARCUS.
> Yes but he …
OSHA.
> You ain't dreaming about me.

MARCUS.
>   No, Osha girl. I don't need you
>   In my dreams. You my friend in
>   Life.
OSHA.
>   I wouldn't be so quick on that one
>   Marc ... Eh boy walk me home.
MARCUS.
>   Osha ...
OSHA.
>   Don't call my name ... Don't call my name ...
>   Don't call me ... Don't ... Don't.
>   Osha exits.
TERRELL.
>   Followed by Terrell.
SHAUNTA IYUN.
>   And Shaunta Iyun too.

A Vision on the Waters

OGUN SIZE.
>   Quiet now Marcus.
MARCUS.
>   I hear it Ogun. I hear it.
>   Marcus moves,
OGUN SIZE.
>   Night.
MARCUS.
>   Night.
OGUN SIZE.
>   Hey ...
MARCUS.
>   Hmm.
OGUN SIZE.
>   What was you and Elegua talking 'bout earlier?
>   Was you really talking 'bout old times?

MARCUS.

I told her … I told her a dream I had.

OGUN SIZE.

Huh, tell it to me. Tell me your dream.

MARCUS.

Marcus stares. I barely remember … But
I remember:

There's this man … and all this rain.

(Lights shift. Oshoosi Size standing in a rain. Humming.)

OSHOOSI SIZE.

Remind him that one day it was raining
Rain came so fast and quick fill up
All the ditches outside and the holes round
The baseball field. Street helping to pour all
This water into the empty spaces filling up
With run-off. And then the sun came out.
Out of nowhere sun just strolled on out
Hot. Every li'l nigga … I'ma try and stop saying that …
Every li'l kid
All
Jump in that water. He just
Stood there watching us; smiling dunking
Under this nasty street made pools. Huh somebody
Say look like the Lord decided these nigg …
These people ain't gone never have nothing
Might as well give 'em something. Gave us
Our own rain made pool. Complete with tetanus
And ringworm. Man, we got out that water
And got to itching. He ain't say nothing.
Ain't get mad just pour that pink thick cream
On me and rub it in 'til I look like I been working
In a chalk mine or 'bout to do a voodoo ritual the one.
He let me get in the water
Knowing I would need him to rub my back when I
Got out.

(Oshoosi sinks down in a pool of water or fades into the screen.)

I done sunk in the dirty water again now. Tell him.
Tell him. Ask him if he remember me.

End of Act One

ACT TWO

Scene 1

OBA.
(Offstage.)
>Marcus Eshu!
>I really do believe you must've lost
>Your true mind boy! Or smacked your
>Forehead on the pavement!

MARCUS.
>Marcus Eshu sits in his room watching
>The walls.

OBA.
(Offstage.)
>I don't
>Care how upset you were or what you
>Were looking to find, you don't bring
>Your behind in here drifting like the
>Morning dew talking 'bout some …

MARCUS.
>He is on punishment for coming home
>So late the other night. He tried to
>Explain to his mother what had happened …

OBA.
(Offstage.)
>Shut up!

MARCUS.
>She was having none of that.

OBA.
>What were you thinking, boy? Enter Oba.
>You know how many boys your age get
>Shot or thrown up in jail 'round here for
>Just walking? Huh? Do you? Answer me!

MARCUS.
>I …

OBA.

>Shut up!
>Sitting 'round here walking the
>Streets like your daddy! You wanna know
>About your daddy he used to walk around
>Too and look what happened to him. Dead
>And in the ground. You want that do you?

MARCUS.

>Tears in her eyes …

OBA.

>You scared the daylights outta me 'round
>Here being fast and grown!
>There's a storm on the way!
>What were you
>Thinking? What did I ever do to make you …

MARCUS.

>Mama …

OBA.

>No! I don't wanna hear nothing
>Out you. I means that Marcus Eshu I do.
>Lord God help me … Oba exits. Talking to
>The Father.

Scene 2

MARCUS.

>Marcus sits in his room staring at the afternoon
>Light.

SHAUNTA IYUN.

>Marcus! Shaunta Iyun enters
>Whispering loud for her friend
>Marcus Eshu!

MARCUS.

>Shaunta what you doing out there girl?

SHAUNTA IYUN.

>I'm doing the Jenny Craig "Call and
>Response workout plan." What it look like I'm

Doing. I'm freeing you like they did
Steven Biko.
MARCUS.
Didn't Steven Biko die in jail?
SHAUNTA IYUN.
Nigga sneak out the house!
MARCUS.
I'm on punishment.
SHAUNTA IYUN.
Thus I said sneak.
C'mon I gotta talk to you about something ...
MARCUS.
I am in enough trouble
As it is. I am not going nowhere with ...
SHAUNTA IYUN.
Ooh you cranky what's wrong with you?
MARCUS.
Gone Shaunta I'm tired.
SHAUNTA IYUN.
You ain't been sleeping?
MARCUS.
Trying not to.
SHAUNTA IYUN.
'Cause of the ...
Huh.
What ... what happens in that dream?
MARCUS.
Nah, last time I went around talking about
What was in my head I ended up wet, tired
And locked in here. Done
Speaking my mind for a li'l while now ...
SHAUNTA IYUN.
But Marcus the rain ...
MARCUS.
Shaunta ...
ELEGUA.
(Offstage. She sings.)
MARCUS.
Marcus hears it.

SHAUNTA IYUN.
　　How could he not?
ELEGUA.
(Offstage. She sings.)
MARCUS.
　　What's that?
ELEGUA.
　　Enter Elegua.
　　Hair undone. Bent low to the ground …
MARCUS.
　　Singing?
SHAUNTA IYUN.
　　Almost screaming.
ELEGUA.
(She sings.)
MARCUS.
　　What's wrong with her Shaunta?
SHAUNTA IYUN.
　　'Swhat I was trying to tell you. A storm coming.
　　Ogun sending Elegua away. Say, she don't need
　　To be out this close to the waters. Say, she can
　　Come back when it's over.
MARCUS.
　　What she walking around screaming for?
SHAUNTA IYUN.
　　She won't say … She won't talk about it with
　　Nobody but ever since you told her about that Dream she
　　Been wandering around crying out like
　　That, going on some days now. She looks to
　　Marcus …
MARCUS.
　　Me? I didn't tell her nothing except …
ELEGUA.
(She sings.)
　　Elegua exits.
SHAUNTA IYUN.
MARCUS.
　　It was just some stupid flick in my forehead.
　　It wasn't nothing to scream about.

SHAUNTA IYUN.

Who you trying to convince?

Don't stay locked up in there forever.

MARCUS.

Where you going Shaunta Iyun?

SHAUNTA IYUN.

To make sure she get home safe.

Shaunta Iyun exits

Scene 3

MARCUS.

Marcus stares after his friend …

SHUA.

Damn you got pretty eyes for a nigga.

MARCUS.

Marcus stunned …

SHUA.

Enter Shua with his Kangol

Low … Down Low.

I mean I'm saying though son the way the

Light playing on your eyes or whatnot, that's

Whatsup though.

MARCUS.

Oh … thank you.

SHUA.

So, yo son what you on?

MARCUS.

Oh, I don't do drugs man.

SHUA.

Word? Are you serious son? You think …

Huh. Country niggas. Yo, I'm trying to

Say yo, you get down?

MARCUS.

Where?

SHUA.

With dudes, son!

MARCUS.

Oh ... oh ... Oh! I mean ...

Oh. Why?

SHUA.

Why else I'ma be asking you?

Come outside.

MARCUS.

I ... Right now?

SHUA.

What, you want the dick later?

MARCUS.

I ... um ... oh ...

Laughing.

My mama ...

SHUA.

Oh your daddy coming too?

MARCUS.

My daddy's dead.

SHUA.

Damn yo! You said that and it was like

"Flame on" in your eyes, son, when you

Talk about your old mans. No disrespect famo.

MARCUS.

What?

SHUA.

My condolences ...

MARCUS.

Thank you ...

SHUA.

How long he been dead for?

MARCUS.

I barely know'd the nig ...

SHUA.

Now don't get sad man. Now the light

Almost gone out your eyes. You want,

If it keep them eyes bright, I let you call

Me daddy.

MARCUS.

Stupid ...

SHUA.
    Serious, man.
    He smiles.
    Come outside.
MARCUS.
    I can't …
SHUA.
    Oh a'ight
    Shua turns to leave …
MARCUS.
    Wait … Meet me. Out by the waters,
    The bayou.
SHUA.
    The swamp?
MARCUS.
    Yeah right off Buras drive.
SHUA.
    How I'ma find you, the light in your eyes?
MARCUS.
    Blush.
    Yeah something … something like
    That. I'm Marcus … What's your …
SHUA.
    Daddy, remember? Call me daddy.

Scene 4

MARCUS.
    Marcus Eshu, sneaking out in the late —
OGUN SIZE.
    Eh Marcus …
Enter Ogun Size.
MARCUS.
    Oh hey!
OGUN SIZE.
    Boy time you try to put things
    Down and you know plant yourself you gotta

Pick up and go. I'm trying to get ready for the
Storm you see.

MARCUS.

I see.

OGUN SIZE.

I'm trying to send Elegua.
Off you know.

MARCUS.

Uh-huh.

OGUN SIZE.

This woman! She keep on wandering off … She ain't slick
I know she ain't senile yet

MARCUS.

Nope.

OGUN SIZE.

Say the storm
Might do make landfall. You never know!
This woman done wandered …
You haven't seen her?

MARCUS.

No.

OGUN SIZE.

I haven't seen you.

MARCUS.

Been on punishment.

OGUN SIZE.

What you doing out?

MARCUS.

Going to meet a friend.

OGUN SIZE.

Oh you …

MARCUS.

A new friend …

OGUN SIZE.

Oh. Oh!

MARCUS.

Smiles.

OGUN SIZE.

Well I gotta find Elegua, listen man, she
Been acting strange ever since …

MARCUS.
Yeah I heard.
OGUN SIZE.
Can you tell the dream again maybe I can …
MARCUS.
I don't remember, I haven't had it …
OGUN SIZE.
The rain in it, is it bad?
MARCUS.
Yeah it gets pretty bad.
OGUN SIZE.
Like bad, bad …
MARCUS.
Bad. To himself, "bad nigga."
OGUN SIZE.
And the man in it?
MARCUS.
Yeah …
OGUN SIZE.
What does he look like?
MARCUS.
Like … I gotta go.
OGUN SIZE.
Eh, didn't you just say you was on punishment
Your mama know …
MARCUS.
Ogun you ain't my daddy man. I mean … You know
You ain't my daddy, I ain't your brother so just …
Gone find your aunt, Ogun. I gotta go.
Marcus exits.

Scene 5

SHUA.
    Night.
MARCUS.
    Sittin' watching the waters.
SHUA.
    Shua with his cap covering his
    Eyes.
MARCUS.
    Marcus with his hands in his lap.
SHUA.
    Shua kisses his teeth.
    Stch!
    How old are you?
MARCUS.
    Sixteen ... I just turned sixteen. You?
SHUA.
    Twenty ... two.
MARCUS.
SHUA.
MARCUS.
    Crickets.
SHUA.
    Shifting.
MARCUS.
    Huh.
SHUA.
    Whatever.
MARCUS.
    Crickets.
SHUA.
    Shua kisses his teeth.
    Stch ...
    So wassup man?
MARCUS.
    Nothing.

SHUA.

I see that. Yo, where you from?

MARCUS.

From here.

SHUA.

Yeah you seem like you from down
Here. Country niggas.
Ey shorty y'all get storms 'round
Here? I was up on the news yo
Say it's one coming.

MARCUS.

Sometimes … Yeah.

SHUA.

Damn yo this my first time down
Here. Visiting my peoples.

MARCUS.

So you're from up north?

SHUA.

From the boogie down baby.

MARCUS.

That's the Bronx right?

SHUA.

Uh-huh. Shua looks o'er
Marcus. Marcus in his jeans
Lookin' just right. You a'ight.

MARCUS.

Thanks.

SHUA.

Yeah you alright. Got a li'l phatty
Or whatnot …

MARCUS.

Thanks …

SHUA.

Them eyes sexy …

MARCUS.

Marcus bites his lips.

SHUA.

Sex lips too … Sexy
Ass lips.

MARCUS.
    Black boy blushing.
SHUA.
    C'mere ...
MARCUS.
    Marcus moves.
SHUA.
    You gonna call me Daddy, Eyes?
    Shua puts his fingers to Marcus' lips.
MARCUS.
    Marcus kisses Shua's fingers.
SHUA.
    Shua moves his hand behind Marcus' head.
MARCUS.
    He pulls Marcus' head down toward
    His lap.
SHUA.
    Lights.

Scene 6

OSHA.
    Osha stomps onto her porch.
    Lord ...
SHUN.
    Shun walking up ...
    Every night, Osha?
OSHA.
    I'm just spending
    Time with him while I can.
SHUN.
    I understand girl I'm just saying give
    Him some time to miss you. You young
    Chicks don't know how to tether niggas.
OSHA.
    He'll miss me when he's gone back
    To the Bronx.

SHUN.

> You need to get him to help put up my storm
> Boards messing round here talking 'bout some, "hanging
> Out." Oh chile never mind. He from up there he
> Don't know nothing 'bout no shutters.
>
> I don't trust them niggas from up there no how.

OSHA.

You rather me be hanging with Marcus.

> Still?

SHUN.

> I didn't mind you … hanging with that boy.
> I just tried to tell you he was his way, like
> That. You know I don't hate on the gays.

OSHA.

> Mama just go in the house.

SHUN.

> Oh hell nah! Get your ass in this house
> He can come ring the doorbell like normal bastards.

OSHA.

> Mama please just let me wait for him by myself.

SHUN.

> Huh. You get yo ass in this house come late night.
> I don't care whicha way a hurricane coming you
> Got school tomorrow. Hear me Osha girl?

OSHA.

> I hear you.

SHUN.

> Shun goes into the house, talking trash.
> Boy come down here talking all side
> Ways. He better just be courting and
> Not trying to do the electric slide with
> My baby I'll light his ass up. I mean that …

Scene 7

MARCUS.
> Enter Marcus Eshu
> She alright?

OSHA.
> You know how she get.

MARCUS.
> How you?

OSHA.
> Alright.

MARCUS.
> You busy or something

OSHA.
> Waiting for a friend …

MARCUS.
> Who? Like … Like a new friend?
> Smiles

OSHA.
> What it matter to you?

MARCUS.
> I ain't come here to fight.

OSHA.
> What you come for?

MARCUS.
> I met a … a friend too. I wanted to
> Tell you.

OSHA.
> Ehuh! Tell Shaunta Iyun she like to hear
> That kind of stuff.

MARCUS.
> Last time I checked you my best too.

OSHA.
> Yeah I thought so too 'til I figured out
> You was lying.

MARCUS.
> Lying!

OSHA.

I didn't stutter man. Lied. You knew Marcus,
Say you didn't, how I was feeling? How
You gone be my best friend and not tell me?
Huh?

MARCUS.

I ...

OSHA.

All you got for me Marcus Eshu? "I."

MARCUS.

Eh gurl, tell me how you didn't
Know I wasn't interested? Huh? Tell me how you
Couldn't tell after all the years after all the teasing
And the fights ... the time you punched Eric down
The way in the stomach cause he called me a faggot?

OSHA.

MARCUS.

He still be running when he see
You coming talking 'Bout some, "gone girl."
When we would play "hide and go-get-it" with the
Other kids. Everybody 'round us hunching and I'm
Talking 'bout some, "let's play cuddle."

OSHA.

I just thought you was being romantic.

MARCUS.

Girl!

OSHA.

Alright. Alright ... I should've known.
I mean you the only one I could sing *The Wiz*
Straight through with.

MARCUS.

(He sings.)

OSHA.

(She sings.)

MARCUS and OSHA.

(They Sing.)

MARCUS.

(He keeps singing.)

SHUA.

Enter Shua Kangol pulled

Way down.
MARCUS and OSHA.
    Hey.
MARCUS.
OSHA.
SHUA.
OSHA.
    You know Joshua?
MARCUS.
    Joshua?
OSHA.
Osha turns to Marcus.
    You met before?
SHUA.
    Shua puts his fingers to his lips.
    To Osha, you ready to go?
MARCUS.
    Huh.
OSHA.
    We'll talk later Marcus.

Scene 8

OBA.
    Oba on the porch.
    I didn't go looking for you 'cause I didn't want to
    Know really where you was. I didn't call for you
    For fear that you might hear me and not answer
    Back.
MARCUS.
OBA.
    I ain't got much to say either Marcus but hear me
    Out. You disobeyed me. The first time you just didn't
    Tell me but this time you heard what I said and still
    You went on your own way. Made your own path.
MARCUS.

70

OBA.

I just want to know where it's leading you?
This sneaking and secrets and lying, and making a
Fool of ... did you really think I didn't know that thick
Girl was hiding you the other night? Where is it
Taking you, Marcus Eshu? You turning into the man
You want to be? Or the man you need to be? Or ...
No matter what you like, or don't, you still a man.
All men have to be men. They say a woman can't
Teach you that ... I got news for you, no man can
Either. Only you can learn it for you.

MARCUS.
OBA.

Gone on in there and lay down ... if you want. I
Can't make you do much a nothing these days.
I figured I would just offer.

MARCUS.

Marcus moves to ...

OBA.

What's this dream I hear you got going?

MARCUS.

Ma'am?

OBA.

Is it something I could ... wanna hear?

MARCUS.

It's something I barely remember.

OBA.

Night.

MARCUS.

Night.

A Dream of Drag

MARCUS.
> That night.
> Marcus is
> Sleeping dreaming this very ... odd, weird dream.
> Not the one ... no this other mess.
> In this dream are the very best friends
> Shaunta Iyun and Osha girl.
> All caught in a sun shower.
> To the best:
> It's raining.

OSHA.
We see that MARCUS.

MARCUS.
> But The sun's out.

SHAUNTA IYUN.
> I see why they put you in the advanced
Class Marcus.

OSHA.
> Them good observation skills

MARCUS.
> Why y'all being so mean!

SHAUNTA IYUN.
> It's raining.

OSHA.
> And you should have told us.

MARCUS.
> I didn't know.

OSHA.
> 'Course you did.

SHAUNTA IYUN.
> It was raining in your dream.

MARCUS.
> Lord first I couldn't get nobody to listen to that
> Stupid dream. Now everybody acting like it King's
> Dream. Look ...

I knew it was raining hard in the dream
But this ain't that. This a sun shower
You know what we used to do in a sun
Shower. Osha, Shaunta Iyun.

BOTH.
Rain …

MARCUS.
Shaunta Iyun going in.
Osha struggling …

OSHA.
Hey!
Ain't we too old to be playing this game.

MARCUS.
Shaunta Iyun giggling …

SHAUNTA IYUN.
This your dreaming Marcus Eshu tell us.

MARCUS.
The song *[He names an old song, funky song.]*
begins to play …

OSHA.
Laughing
Oh hell to nah.

SHAUNTA IYUN.
We are not …

MARCUS.
Yes we are …
Shaunta pats her weave.

OSHA.
Are you …

SHAUNTA IYUN.
For real?

OSHA.
This was cute when we were kids Marcus.

MARCUS.
Osha rocks back on her heels.

OSHA.
But we grown now …

MARCUS.
She puts her hand on her hip.

SHAUNTA IYUN.

Back then they would call it kids being
Cute.

OSHA.

When you grown —

SHAUNTA IYUN.

They call it a drag show.

MARCUS.

It's my dream. We gone do what I want.
All laughing and playing in the rain.

SHAUNTA IYUN.

Ha! So you dream of drag now?

MARCUS.

Maybe guess we have to wait and see

OSHA.

Lord you are so free and easy in your dreams
Marcus Eshu

MARCUS.

Nah not always only when I'm with you
Two ...

ALL THREE.

My best.

MARCUS.

C'mon y'all sing the song.

ALL THREE.

(They sing.)

MARCUS.

Osha singing lead

OSHA.

(She sings.)

MARCUS.

Madam Iyun

SHAUNTA IYUN.

(She sings.)

ALL THREE.

(They sing.)

MARCUS.

Taking over ...

(He sings.)

BOTH.
 Sang Marcus Eshu
MARCUS.
(He sings.)
SHUA.
MARCUS.
 The Music stops. We stop dancing.
 What you want?
SHUA.
MARCUS.
 Rain pours … the sun is
 Gone.
 My friends are gone. To Shua.
 Get out of my dream.
 Shua smiles.
 Shua takes off his Kangol. He strips down
 And now he looks like …
OSHOOSI SIZE.
 Oshoosi Size dressed in all white …
 Shh! Shh! It's gone be okay.
 Shh now Marcus. It's gone be alright …
 Just ask him ask my Ogun.
 For me.

Scene 9

MARCUS.
 The next morning:
 Black boy running …
 Mama?
OBA.
 Oba still on the porch.
MARCUS.
 Mama?
OBA.
MARCUS.
 Mama I … I will be right back. I have to tell

Osha and Shaunta …
OBA.
Do what you please, Marcus.
MARCUS.
I will be right back.
OBA.
What you please.
MARCUS.
When I come back let me in.
OBA.
She goes in.
MARCUS.
He runs out.

Scene 10

SHAUNTA IYUN.
Enter Shaunta Iyun eating a sandwich singing
Why everything supposed to be bad make me
Feel so good?
MARCUS.
Thank you Father! Shaunta
SHAUNTA IYUN.
Boy what you doing? What's wrong you coming
'Round the corner breathing like the big girls?
MARCUS.
Shaunta I gotta tell you something …
SHAUNTA IYUN.
Oh now you ready to tell me something.
Wait a dream?
MARCUS.
No … well yeah.
SHAUNTA IYUN.
It's about me and Jason Witt?
MARCUS.
What?
SHAUNTA IYUN.
Shaunta braving.

I know! I know! I should have told you …
But it's hard to come out and be like, "I like, have
Loved this white boy since the third grade!"
MARCUS.
Shaunta Iyun.
SHAUNTA IYUN.
But he so cute and nice and country as hell …
MARCUS.
I sucked Shua's dick.
SHAUNTA IYUN.
Shaunta Iyun drops her sandwich.
MARCUS.

SHAUNTA IYUN.
Shua?
MARCUS.
Yes.
SHAUNTA IYUN.
Josh ua …
MARCUS.
Nods.
SHAUNTA IYUN.
That fake-ass neyo kat with the Usher hat?
Shaunta Iyun swats her foolish friend.
The one that's Osha seeing!
MARCUS.
Eh gurl!
SHAUNTA IYUN.
What you suck his dick for! All the
Dick in the world and you gotta suck
His!
MARCUS.
Ain't like I knew she was dating him. She
And me weren't talking and his ass ain't say shit
'Cept yeah that feel good.
SHAUNTA IYUN.
Least you know you good at it.
MARCUS.
Shaunta!

SHAUNTA IYUN.

Identify your strengths

MARCUS.

We gotta tell her.

SHAUNTA IYUN.

We!

MARCUS.

We just gone let him keep lying to her?

SHAUNTA IYUN.

Uh-uh oh no ma'am. I don't like how you got Creole all the
sudden

Marcus E. Throwing all this here "we" in the soup. *We*

Didn't give the king of New York some face. *We*

Weren't there to watch it and now *we* gone act like

We don't know nothing 'bout it. Starting right, Shaunta looks

At her imaginary watch, now.

MARCUS.

Shaunta Iyun …

SHAUNTA IYUN.

Eh there Marcus E. Baby BABY! What's going on man

How's that secret of sweet coming? I don't nothing about

No homoerotic fellatio. Nope. Not me. Couldn't be! Then

who!

MARCUS.

You right no sense in her killing us both.

SHAUNTA IYUN.

Tell her you didn't mean to suck it.

MARCUS.

A realization.

Just bring her out by the waters?

SHAUNTA IYUN.

What?

MARCUS.

Yeah just bring her out there.

SHAUNTA IYUN.

Huh.

There goes a brave man.

Shaunta Iyun exits.

Damn boy made me drop my sandwich.

A Re-Collection

I'm old enough to know better. To know. What did
I expect to happen, did you see this coming? Huh, you could-
n'ta …
Guess I wouldn't've listened or heard but
I hear now. Yessuh. I do. I hear you can't just wake up one
morning
A dream on your mind, in your heart, spend that day
No matter whose wedding or funeral running 'round
Telling everybody 'bout it. Just talking I got a dream
It went like this … I got this feeling feels like this …
Lesson: When you thought about it
Prayed about it and you can't keep it to yourself …
Maybe it's better to run or walk away but don't give
It unto the air.
You realize that your dreams too heavy for
Everyone else? You can grin; you can bare 'em but the world
Seem to light a fire or drown deep when you mention
Your innermost thoughts, wishes, desire … so what's that
teaching: Keep it
To yourself? That ain't right either.
So how do you play it?
How does this run out? 'Cause right now I'm back out here
By the waters knowing more than I did, understanding
    … Well I'm still standing but just barely
My best friends 'bout to hate me.
Got a ol' lady say she see a storm somehow in my dream and
A mama who barely can look me in the eye cause she think
I'm
On the ho' stroll and she ain't but half wrong, she ain't but
half Wrong
'Cause I'm out here again waiting under the good Gods sky
for Some up
North down low negro and …
These dreams.
All I got are these dreams and memories. The dream of a

man who
I think … well I know … but how to tell that part? How to explain That …
Stop thinking Marcus just tell him.
'Cause all that thinking this thinking ain't gone undo
Redo make do nothing. Time to quit thinking or quicker think so
The next move is made before the thought. The next move don't
Take a whole lot of thought. The next move … Here he comes.
Here we go. Marcus moves.

Scene 12

SHUA.
    Enter Shua. Kangol: Low
    You know. 'Sup yo?
MARCUS.
    Heavy Breath …
    Hey.
SHUA.
    Evening, as y'all say.
MARCUS.
    Huh that's funny, you funny, you
    Always been funny?
SHUA.
    You alright man?
MARCUS.
    Oh I'm fine. Yeah I mean
    Sexy: I'm fine.
SHUA.
    Laughing. Yeah alright.
    What you stepping up?
MARCUS.
    Yeah I am … yo.
SHUA.
    Huh.

MARCUS.
 You … you like that?
SHUA.
 Your gurl know what went down
 Between us?
MARCUS.
 Uh-uh.
SHUA.
 So what you trying to keep this going
 On the side, right?
MARCUS.
 Um … yeah
SHUA.
 That's whats' …
MARCUS.
 I mean no …
 Marlene Dietrich:
 I think I might be the jealous type.
SHUA.
 Like that? You get green …
MARCUS.
 Lauren Bacall:
 Yeah, I like to keep my friends to myself.
SHUA.
 Shit that's cool 'n' th' gang baby.
 I mean long as you can keep a secret.
MARCUS.
(To us.)
 Is he for real?
 Yeah I'm good at keeping my mouth shut.
 People 'round here don't even know about me.
SHUA.
 Ha! Oh yeah?
MARCUS.
 Yeah …
SHUA.
 Well this time we ain't got to worry about your mouth.
MARCUS.
 Huh?

SHUA.

I 'on't need your lips.

MARCUS.

What you doing?

SHUA.

I bet you tight.

MARCUS.

Hol' up …

SHUA.

Touch.

MARCUS.

Eh man!

SHUA.

That's it. That's them eyes lightening up.

MARCUS.

Just back up …

SHUA.

Touch,

You making me hot, son.

MARCUS.

Please …

SHUA.

You give good ass?

MARCUS.

I ain't never … Gone man!

SHUA.

GRAB!

Can't.

Your eyes calling me.

Shua moves to …

MARCUS.

Get off me!

(They struggle.)

SHAUNTA IYUN.

C'mon —

OSHA.

Stop girl …

SHUA.

C'mon let me get that ass nigga!

OSHA.
Joshua get your hands off him!
SHUA.
Shua stops.
Realizing
Oh so y'all kats trying to play me. Put my
Business out there like that? Trying to put
My shit on blast …
SHAUNTA IYUN.
Nah you trying to put your shit on boys did that!
SHUA.
Shut the fuck up …
MARCUS.
Marcus moves.
Uh.
(He punches Shua.)
OSHA.
Gone Joshua, just gone.
SHUA.
Shua holding his face.
Fuck this … Fuck this …
Exit Shua.
MARCUS.
Osha …
OSHA.
What?
MARCUS.
I wanted to … wanted to tell you.
OSHA.
You told me …
MARCUS.
I'm … I'm sorry.
OSHA.
Me too.
MARCUS.
I love you.
OSHA.
Me too.
Osha exits.

MARCUS.
    Tears …
SHAUNTA IYUN.
    Roll down his face.
    Marcus?
MARCUS.
    Hm?
SHAUNTA IYUN.
    You ain't crying 'cause she left huh?
(He shakes his head.)
    You crying 'cause punching that boy
    Hurt your damn hand.
(He nods.)
    Laughing. Awww. Shhh! Shhh! It's gone be
    Okay. Shhh now Marcus it's gone be alright …
MARCUS.
    Marcus steps back.
SHAUNTA IYUN.
    Like he just heard a ghost.
MARCUS.
    Or remembered a …

Epilogue

MARCUS.
    Marcus stands on Elegua's porch wanting to
    Knock but her windows are all boarded up.
OGUN SIZE.
    She ain't home.
Enter Ogun Size.
    She left to Houston finally. Be back
    When the storm passes. Ogun Size turns
    To go.
MARCUS.
    You know dreams, Ogun?
OGUN SIZE.
    Ogun stops.

MARCUS.

I have this dream.

OGUN SIZE.

I know your dream.

MARCUS.

But I didn't tell it right before.
In the dream is your brother Ogun.
Your brother comes to me in this dream
At first I didn't know what to tell you
Or what he was saying But he come to me
And he tell me to say, remind you, he say
To tell you tell my brother …

MARCUS and OSHOOSI SIZE.

Tell my brother Ogun.

OSHOOSI SIZE.

Enter Oshoosi Size.

Tell my brother that the nights I cried were
Because I dreamt he wasn't there when
I woke up. Tell him that he never had to run
Far to get me I was always right where he put
Me. Tell him tell him the the sky is 'bout
To open up, and God's gone open His eye wide
Over the bayou and the sky will cry for and
Spread His pool of teardrops wider over the
Earth. I done sunk down already now. Already
Down in that dirty water. All that is … was.
Tell him …

MARCUS and OSHOOSI SIZE.

Tell him.

OGUN SIZE.

Father …

MARCUS.

You believe, Ogun?

OGUN SIZE.

No choice but to …

MARCUS.

What it mean, Ogun? What my dream mean?

OGUN SIZE.

Ogun Size can't help hearing all that Marcus.

Eshu say.

MARCUS.
    He looks to the sky.
OGUN SIZE.
    Finds all the answers there. It means …
    It means my brother's dead.
    You dream like your daddy
    and I'm … I'm tired
    Just now.
MARCUS.
    Ogun Size marches a funeral processional by himself
OGUN SIZE.
    Walk with me lord …
    Walk with me …
    Walk with me Lord …
    Walk with me …
(Ogun walks in a mock processional all his own.)
MARCUS.
    Marcus stares after Ogun
    To make sure he gets home safe.

End of Play

PROPERTY LIST

Large black umbrella
Sandwich

SOUND EFFECTS

Gunshot
Rain
Music

NOTES
(Use this space to make notes for your production)